ECLECTIC EDUCATIONAL SERIES.

McGUFFEY'S

NEWLY REVISED

ECLECTIC PRIMER.

WITH PICTORIAL ILLUSTRATIONS.

WILDSIDE PRESS

ROMAN NUMERALS EXPLAINED.

A numeral is a symbol meaning number. Our system of counting is believed to have begun by people counting on their fingers. Both the Arabic (1, 2, 3, 4, etc.) and the Roman (I, II, III, IV, etc.) are believed to have started this way. The word digit, meaning number, is from the Latin word digitus, meaning finger. The number V (5) seems to be representative of an open hand; and, the number X (10) seems to be like two open hands.

In earlier days, our forefathers used the Roman system to indicate chapter headings in books. To help you understand those numbers more easily you may refer to the chart below:

Roman	Arabic	Roman	Arabic	Roman	Arabic
I	1	XI	11	XXX	30
II	2	XII	12	XL	40
III	3	XIII	13	L	50
IV	4	XIV	14	LX	60
V	5	XV	15	LXX	70
VI	6	XVI	16	LXXX	80
VII	7	XVII	17	XC	90
VIII	8	XVIII	18	C	100
IX	9	XIX	19	D	500
X	10	XX	20	M	1000

Entered according to Act of Congress, in the year 1849,
By WINTHROP B. SMITH,
In the Clerk's Office of the District Court
of the United States for the District of Ohio.

PREFACE.

This small volume, intended as a first book for children, will, it is hoped, be found an acceptable aid to little learners in their earliest efforts to ascend the ladder of learning.

SIMPLICITY.—The lessons contain the most simple words—those with which the EAR of the child is familiar. By the combination of these words in easy sentences, connected with pleasing and impressive *pictures*, it is designed at once to fix the attention and to interest the mind, and in this way to make the lessons a medium for imparting *ideas* to the child.

PROGRESSION.—A careful progression has been preserved, thus leading the little learner forward, step by step, by an easy gradation, which, while it pleases, will at the same time instruct him in the use and meaning of language.

SPELLING.—Many of the words in the spelling exercises are very often repeated, that the pupil may *frequently* spell them. Every *teacher* is aware that *repetition* is necessary in instructing young children in this branch.

This book is intended as an introduction to "McGuffey's Eclectic First Reader."

☞ The Pictorial Illustrations in this Primer, have, with but few exceptions, been designed and engraved expressly for it, and a copyright for them has been legally secured by the publishers.

ALPHABET.

a	A	*a*	n	N	*n*
b	B	*b*	o	O	*o*
c	C	*c*	p	P	*p*
d	D	*d*	q	Q	*q*
e	E	*e*	r	R	*r*
f	F	*f*	s	S	*s*
g	G	*g*	t	T	*t*
h	H	*h*	u	U	*u*
i	I	*i*	v	V	*v*
j	J	*j*	w	W	*w*
k	K	*k*	x	X	*x*
l	L	*l*	y	Y	*y*
m	M	*m*	z	Z	*z*

	AX. ax.
	BOX. box.
	CAT. cat.
	DOG. dog.
	ELK. elk.

FAN.
fan.

GIRL.
girl.

HEN.
hen.

INK.
ink.

JUG.
jug.

KID.
kid.

LARK.
lark.

MAN.
man.

NUT.
nut.

OX.
ox.

PIG.
pig.

QUAIL.
quail.

RAT.
rat.

SUN.
sun.

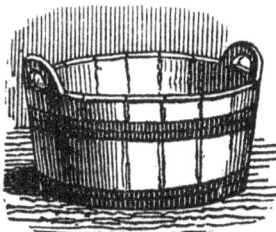

TUB.
tub.

URN.
urn.

VINE.
vine.

WREN.
wren.

X.
x.

YOKE.
yoke.

ZEBRA.
zebra.

LESSON I.

Spelling.

is	it	an	ox
it	is	an	ox
it	is	my	ox

Reading.

Is it an ox?

It is an ox.

It is my ox.

Spelling.

	do	we	go	
	do	we	go	up
	we	do	go	up

Reading.   Do we go?

Do we go up?

We do go up.

Spelling.

	am	I	in		
	am	I	in	it	
	I	am	in	it	
	so	is	he	in	it

Reading.   Am I in?

Am I in it?

I am in it.

So is he in it.

LESSON II.*

Is it an ax?

It is an ax.

It is my ax.

It is by me.

So it is!

I go to it.

---

* Let the child spell each word in the line: then read, as in Lesson I.

Am I in? No.

Is he in?

He is in.

I am by him.

Do you go in?

We do go in.

It is I.

It is we.

It is he.

We do it.

Do as we do.

I do as you do.

LESSON III.*

A fat pig,
can not run.

A brown cow.
Has she hay?

See the kid.
It can run.

A sly fox,
had a hen.

---

* Let the child spell each word in the line: then
read, as in Lesson I.

An old ape.
Can he hop?

See the rat.
It was hid.

Let the cat,
get the rat.

A red ox.
Let him go.

LESSON IV.*

A sly hen.
She can fly.

See the elk.
It can run.

A red dog.
It bit a pig.

See the bat.
It can fly.

---

* Let the child spell each word in the line: then read, as in Lesson I.

LESSON V.

I see a pig.
How fat is it!
Can the pig run?
It can not run.
It is too fat.

Is it a cow?

It is a cow.

It is my cow.

She has no hay.

Let her be fed.

LESSON VI.

See my fat ox.

Is it an old ox?

It is an old ox.

Not a red ox.

It is a brown ox.

I see a nag.

Do you see it?

Yes, yes, I do.

The nag can run.

See it, see it.

LESSON VII.

Oh! see the fly.

How it can fly!

It bit an ox.

The fly can run.

Run, fly, run.

A sly old ape.

It has a nut.

Get it for me.

May I get it?

Yes, if you can.

LESSON VIII.

See my new top.
How it can hum.
You may get one.
Do not beg one.
I do not beg.

See! a new cap.

A cap for you.

I had a cap.

It was new.

Now it is old.

LESSON IX.

An old log hut.

A new log hut.

Is it for me?

Is it for you?

Why do you ask?

I see a tub.

The tub is big.

Can you use it?

Oh yes, I can.

I can use it.

LESSON X.

Is it a bed?

It is a bed.

Is it for you?

It is for me.

Kit is on my bed.

Old Tom, our cat.

He is ill in bed.

Tom saw a rat.

The rat saw Tom.

The rat ran away.

LESSON XI.

It is an elk.

The elk is sly.

The dog saw him.

He saw the dog,

and he ran away.

See the big kid.
It is a pet.
It is not shy,
but it is merry.
Let us go out.

LESSON XII.

See the dog run.
It saw a man.
The man did say,
pup, pup, pup,
and the dog ran.

A sly old fox.
A fat old hen.
The fox did try,
to get the hen.
The hen did fly.

LESSON XIII.

so	see	me	far
oh	yes	you	hop
ah	can	Ned	Tom

Ned, can you hop?

Yes, I can hop.

I can hop so far.

Can you hop, Tom?

Oh yes! See me.

Ah! so you can.

LESSON XIV.

as	six	you	ten
am	old	why	but
are	big	how	Ann

Ann, how old are you?

I am six.

Are you but six?

Why, I am ten.

You are as big as I am.

LESSON XV.

get	the	did	how
sly	see	has	you
yes	far	run	now

Can the dog get the rat?

Yes, he can get the rat.

See! see, how sly he is.

Now he has the rat.

Did you see the rat run?

The dog did not let it run far.

LESSON XVI.

if	let	fat	bit
us	fed	sty	now
go	pig	not	and

I see a dog. A dog bit my pig.

Let us go and see if my pig is in the sty.

The dog can not see my pig now.

Let the fat old pig be fed.

LESSON XVII.

A fan for Ann.

Can you fan me?

I can fan you.

You can fan me,

and you do.

I see you, cat.

Do you see me?

The cat is on
my new fur cap.

Get off, old cat.

LESSON XVIII.

pin				jay
bit				pay
kit				say
sin				day
din	tin	fit	mit	hay
fin	win	hit	pit	may

bad				bed
lad				fed
joy				led
boy				ned
coy	how	gad	pad	red
toy	now	had	sad	wed

LESSON XIX.

I see a dog.

I see a pup.

Do you see me?

The dog and pup,

may run all day.

I see a cat.
The old cat
is by her pet kit.
The cat and kit
are on a rug.

LESSON XX.

rat	hat	cat	bat	mat
dug	bug	hug	jug	mug
sat	vat	fog	dog	pug

nag	tag	lag	hag	rag
ran	pan	tan	van	man
in	at	of	ax	off

LESSON XXI.

Sly	fly	bee
fox	out	old
fed	had	bud
him	how	hum
you	Ann	Tom

Do you see Ann and Tom?
A dog is by Tom and Ann.
It is Sly.
Sly is a big dog.
Do you see him?
He is fed by Tom and Ann.

A bee can hum.
Do you see the bee?
The bee is on a bud.
The bee can fly.

LESSON XXII.

too
pet
pig
was

| Hal | box | boy | Ned |
| odd | bad | but | who |

Ned had a pet pig.

Was it not an odd pet?

Hal had a pet hen.

It was an odd pet too.

Ned, who had the pig, was a bad boy.

Hal, the boy who had the hen, was a big boy, but not a bad boy.

LESSON XXIII.

us	day	out
we	hay	fun
put	our	new

It is a hot day. Let us go out.

Let us go with our dog, to the new cut hay.

We can put hay on our dog for fun. Let us go.

LESSON XXIV.

off	cat	sat
box	boy	lid
eye	ran	bid
and	got	put

A boy put a cat in a box.

A hen was in the box.

The boy sat on the lid of the box.

The cat bit the hen, and the hen put out the eye of the cat.

The boy got off the lid of the box.

The cat got out and ran away.

LESSON XXV.

in	as	the	sun
ill	but	hay	too
up	get	hen	was

The hen was too ill to get up, but not so ill as to die.

The hen was put on the hay, in the sun.

LESSON XXVI.

one
lap
she
sit
his
are
all
yet

lie   ear   out   her

Ann had a pet lap dog.

She let it lie on her bed.

She fed it all she had to eat.

It was not as big as a kid one day old.

The tip of one ear was red, and it had one red leg.

LESSON XXVII.

the	did	paw	Ann
as	tip	put	bid
its	red	and	was

One day, Ann told her dog to put its red paw on her lap.

The dog did as it was told, and put only the red paw on her lap.

LESSON XXVIII.

bed	off	hat	put	may
sod	ill	let	our	boy
old	too	cot	out	the
die	run	not	new	thy
lie	hop	but	dew	why

The sun is up.

Let us go out.

Get my new hat.

Can we run to the cot?

If we can, we may see the boy who is ill.

He can not go out, and run and hop, as we can.

He is ill, too ill to get off the bed.

---

sot	mad	fig	mug
lot	had	gig	tug
sex	sad	rig	sop
vex	rod	wig	cup

LESSON XXIX.

hen
pen
din
pad
bad
led   fed   red   bed   lag

man
lad
sod
boy
men
pet   bet   bat   mat   rug

LESSON XXX.

hog
log
joy
sod
bud
dew

fox
cut
box
did
bid
big

bend	vend	fond	bulb
tend	lend	bond	bald
mend	spend	fund	bard
rand	wind	stand	hard

LESSON XXXI.

Tom
Day
Ned
Ray
was
mad

one   cry   see   bad   ear   sad

Tom Day was a bad boy.

One day, bad Tom Day bit the ear of Ned Ray. Ned did not cry.

Tom Day did cry. Tom was angry.

It was sad to see such a boy as Tom Day.

LESSON XXXII.

Mary
Lucy
why
now
day
you

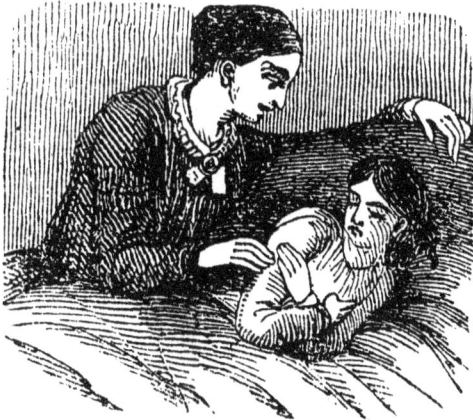

up lie bed and six get

Get up, Lucy. Do not lie in bed now.

It is day, and the sun is up.

Mary got up at six, and is out now.

Up, up, Lucy, why do you lie in bed!

Get up, Lucy, and go out to Mary.

LESSON XXXIII.

cat	do	the	say
lie	fly	sip	sly
lap	and	may	mew

The cat may say, I do not sip, I lap.

I can get a fly, or a rat. I can run.

I can mew, and I can lie in the sun.

all	me	see	eat
cat	try	run	rat
get	but	her	can

The rat may say, I eat all I can get.

The cat may try to get me, but if I see her I run.

me	am	sly	had
his	fat	old	saw
hid	fox	ran	man

The fox may say, I am sly.

I had an old fat hen. A man and his dog saw me. I ran and hid.

LESSON XXXIV.

oh	air	fit
not	aid	all
our	for	we
God	has	eye

Oh my God! Do not allow me to sin. Help me to do as I am told.

Let me do unto others as I would have them do unto me. Our God can see all we do.

God has an ear to all we say.

Let all I do, be fit for His eye.

LESSON XXXV.

sin	eye	one	can
his	did	you	who
see	but	may	men

God can see all.

Who can see God? Not one.

Do not sin, for God can see you.

Men may not see you, but the eye of God is on you.

LESSON XXXVI.*

SPELL.		PRONOUNCE.
li	on	lion
ox	en	oxen
Ab	by	Abby
Lu	cy	Lucy
Ma	ry	Mary
po	et	poet

* Teachers are aware that many words of four letters in two syllables, are deemed more simple than some monosyllables of three letters; for example, *eye*, *ear, than, who, why, eat*, &c., are more difficult words than those in lessons 36 and 37.

SPELL.		PRONOUNCE.
po	ny	pony
bo	ny	bony
di	al	dial
du	ty	duty
he	ro	hero
ru	in	ruin

LESSON XXXVII.

SPELL.		PRONOUNCE.
la	dy	lady
ho	ly	holy
pu	ny	puny
ro	sy	rosy

SPELL.		PRONOUNCE.
ba	by	baby
i	cy	icy
fu	el	fuel
re	al	real

LESSON XXXVIII.

air	fly	off
bee	tea	my
dew	bud	sip
why	may	cup

Do you see my cup? A bee is in it.

Why did the bee get in the cup?

My cup is not for a bee.

The bee got into the cup to sip the tea.

Sip and fly away bee. Fly out into the air.

Get in the cup of the bud, and sip of its dew.

LESSON XXXIX.

wagon	clover	Henry
table	rover	Susan
stable	handle	Nancy
able	candle	very
robin	paper	solar
over	caper	after
kitten	taper	under
puppy	Peter	carpet

LESSON XL.

cows
pigs
dogs
boys
hens
pens
old

sold   fold   cold   hold   bold

rose
tall
fall
call
ball
wall
tell

fell   sell   bell   dell   well

LESSON XLI.

Lucy
Ann
new
said
has
cover

the box see was big you

Lucy has a new box, a big box.

Let us go and see it. The box is red.

Lucy said it was for her:

So, Ann, it can not be for you.

It has an L on the cover: L for Lucy.

LESSON XLII.

boy
tree
rose
nest
mice
cake
get
bell   bite   eggs   pray   made

bird
cage
feet
first
hand
band
hill
feel   reel   heel   rest   hide

LESSON XLIII.

Ned
why
how
soon
down
red
get
setting   out   sun   cap   will

May I get my cap?

Ned, we can go and see the sun set.

See how red it is!

Why is the setting sun so red?

It will soon be down.

LESSON XLIV.

age
lad
boy
man
met
two
said

add cow make little driving

An old man met a little boy driving a cow. The old man said, "My lad, how old are you?"

The boy said, "Sir, if you add two to my age, it will make ten."

LESSON XLV.

too	may	let	wet
sun	dry	not	dew
out	hot	but	now
	Lucy	Mary	

It is too wet now for Lucy and Mary to go out, but the hot sun can dry up the dew, and by and by, Lucy and Mary may go out.

LESSON XLVI.

away	cord	rule	today
rope	same	mule	sitting
cart	band	hill	dinner
dart	hand	mill	trying
buff	land	fill	mister
muff	sand	pill	summer
cuff	told	rill	hungry

One summer day, a hungry fox saw a fat hen, sitting on a box lid.

The fox saw the boy. "Ah!" said he, "I can not get a dinner today.

"If I am not off, the boy may get me." So, away ran the fox.

The sly fox said, "I can get a dinner now," but not so.

A big boy saw mister Fox, as he was trying to get the hen, and ran for his gun.

LESSON XLVII.

fish
wish
dish
miss
hiss
bold
cold
mind

kind   found   bush   push

deer
and
buck
rack
crop
bent
sent
send

back   hack   lack   pack

LESSON XLVIII.

ears
eyes
bell
had
were
little

bit   son   saw   old   cut
one   was   man   dim   why

An old man was ill, and his eyes were dim. I saw him led by a dog.

It was a little red dog. One of its ears was cut, or bit.

Why was the old man led by a dog? Had he no son? He had not.

LESSON XLIX.

Jack
tail
hoof
mane
draw
corn
born   horn   barn   morn

well
dark
deep
peep
drop
rail
pail   bail   nail   mail

LESSON L.

sat		owl
say		shot
oak		had
said		tree
gun		after
saw		sunset

An owl sat in the top of an oak tree.

The owl can not see by day.

It can see after sunset.

A boy saw the owl, and said to a man, "An owl is in the oak."

The man got his gun, and shot at the owl.

LESSON LI.

vine
wine
crib
corn
plum
rice
ripe   rain   pain   bind

melon
apple
berry
collar
butter

LESSON LII.

see	rat	the	will
and	ran	she	has
hay	yes	one	out
cat	saw	had	how

I saw the cat, out by the hay.

She ran as if she saw a rat.

If it is a rat, she will get it.

Let us go and see if she has one.

Yes, she has a rat, a big one.

Oh! Do see how fat the rat is.

LESSON LIII.

molehill
barnyard
cornmeal
nailhead
doorstep
woodpile

rabbit
raven
eagle
martin
hornet
runner

LESSON LIV.

pen
cap
its
saw

out	one	his	only
pig	two	has	little
sty	boy	new	going

See the boy. It is little Ned.

Ned has a new cap. He is going to the sty, or pen, to see his pig.

I saw it fed at one. It is now only two.

The pig can not get out of its pen.

LESSON LV.

farmer
riding
raking
taking
driving
mowing

cripple
ample
simple
dimple
sample
dapple

LESSON LVI.

try
out
use
can
eel   see   saw   mud
low   you   may   again

I saw an eel in the mud.

I tried to get it, but did not get it.

May I try again? There is no need to try. You can not get it.

It is low in the mud, you can not see it.

LESSON LVII.

plum
peach
teach
drum
reach each care dare
pain gain mire fire

rose
nose
hose
seem
seen salt malt halt
feed tell sell well

LESSON LVIII.

may
but
you
now
will
why

| do | my | the | are | bid |
| am | kit | cat | ask | her |

Leave the cat alone. She has a kit.

Do not go to her now.

Why may I not go to her now?

Do not ask why, but do as you are told.

I will do as I am told.

LESSON LIX.

bark	will	ant
air	big	you
puss	purr	dish
old	paw	from
afraid	away	flying
	eating	

As a pup was eating from a dish, it saw a bee and an ant.

The bee was not on a bud, but was flying in the air.

The ant did not fly. An ant can not fly, but it can run.

The pup put its paw on the ant, and ran away from the bee.

It was a big bee, and the pup was afraid.

A pup will try to bark like a dog.

A dog will lie on a mat, or a rug.

Puss will purr, if I let her lie on my lap.

Puss is not afraid of the pup, but she is afraid of the old dog.

LESSON LX.

bird
nest
eggs
bill

wing	sing	ring	king
legs	sings	rings	kings

cage
rage
page
sage

life	wife	fork	cork
fife	ball	call	fall

LESSON LXI.

dog
was
him
eye
saw
pen
pig

why	dog	was	him
Ann	hand	sister	sitting

A dog bit the hand of my sister Ann.

Why did the dog do that? Ann was sitting by him, and was kind to him.

I saw him go by the pen. His eye was on the pig. But the pig was not bit.

LESSON LXII.

mouse
trap
pump
spin

| come | book | look | took |
| play | pray | bray | gray |

bee
hive
some
feed

| home | coop | hoop | name |
| need | dove | love | ride |

LESSON LXIII.

A dog saw a rat.

The cat saw the rat.

They ran for it.

But the cat got it.

Why did not the dog get it?

Ah! The cat was hid, and as the rat got out of a box, she put her paw on it.

Will she kill it? Yes, she will.

LESSON LXIV.

kite
rise
lift
long
lost
boys
girls   dogs   hens   pigs

mill
fill
best
west
rest
beak
leak   rang   sang   hang

LESSON LXV.

pups	ran	did
saw	run	dog
was	can	yes
here	and	fast

I saw an old dog and a pup.

The pup was not as big as the dog.

The old dog ran, and so did the pup.

Can a pup run?

Yes, a pup can run, all pups can run.

A pup can not run as fast as a dog.

Here is a pup with a big dog.

LESSON LXVI.

duck
drake
nice
fine
drink   sleep   small
stray   large   kite

goose
gander
gosling
wing
pond   swim   hiss
river   flying   swimmer

LESSON LXVII.

here	with	you
hold	gave	new
held	when	rose
went	then	line

Here is Tom with his new kite.

Tom said to little Ned, "See my kite!

Let us go and fly it. When it is up in the air, you may then hold the line."

Ned went with Tom, and held the kite.

Tom ran, and the kite rose.

Then Tom gave the line to Ned.

LESSON LXVIII.

bird	tree	nest
four	lost	took
plum	want	were
eggs	seems	sorry

The bird has lost her nest.

See how sad and sorry she seems.

Little Sam Page saw the nest in a plum tree, and took it.

Did Sam want the nest?

No. He took it for the four eggs that were in it. Was he not a bad boy?

LESSON LXIX.

was
boy
like
poor
once
then

went weak strong
brave young little

See the old man. He is weak and poor.

Once he was a little boy like you.

Once he was a young man, and strong, and brave.

Now he is old, and ill, and poor.

LESSON LXX.

wax	she	eyes	Jane
this	lips	shoes	Page
girl	doll	went	brown
gave	Day	small	little
blue	hair	cheeks	Susan

Little Jane Day has a big new doll.

She went to see Susan Page, and Susan gave her this doll.

It is a wax doll, and has red lips and cheeks, and blue eyes.

It has brown hair, and red shoes.

Jane has a small box to put it in.

LESSON LXXI.

her
long
left
fall
poor
took
hold
broke

Sam
where

room
broken

Poor Jane! Her doll is broken.

Little Sam Page was in the room, where Jane had left her doll, and took it.

He did not hold it long, but let it fall, and now it is broken.

LESSON LXXII.

cock
rock
back
hack

| flock | dock | lock | sock |
| tack | lack | pack | rack |

setter
better
hatter
matter

| play | bray | letter | fetter |
| tray | stray | dray | pray |

LESSON LXXIII.

long	dark	horse
trot	your	take
move	come	small
head	well	tail
eyes	must	carry
	stable	

I like this horse. I like his long tail, and small head, and dark eyes.

Come, sir, trot a little, I must see you move. So! you carry your tail well; your head is up. Take him to the stable, and let him be fed.

LESSON LXXIV.

ah	this	goes
bee	thing	rests
rose	bird	rises
come	wing	sister
glossy	golden	settles
	shining	

Oh, see! Oh, see! This shining thing!

It rests its golden glossy wing.

Sister, sister, come and see!

It's not a bird, it's not a bee.

Ah! It rises! Up it goes.

Now it settles on a rose.

LESSON LXXV.

oh	Ann	with
hat	will	shut
book	your	when
back	come	went
very	happy	ready
	mother	

Ann, you may shut your book. We will go out now. Ann put on her hat, and then she ran for her pet dog.

When she came back, her mother was ready, and Ann went with her.

Oh, how happy she was!

LESSON LXXVI.

since	have	catch
steal	mice	closed
dear	sings	moment
harm	wakes	morning

Look at Puss and our bird. If Puss gets the bird, she will kill and eat it.

Puss may catch the mice, for they steal, and do us harm.

Puss must not have our dear bird, that sings to us, and wakes us when it is morning.

LESSON LXXVII.

Ah! See sly Puss!

She is lying on the rug.

Her eyes are closed, but she is not sleeping.

A moment since, her eyes were open.

She saw our bird, and if she can, she will get it.

Oh! Do not let Puss get our bird.

LESSON LXXVIII.

sheep
creep
peep
keep
sleep   grass   shall   words
lamb   glass   while   past

deer
beer
hare
care
pare   haste   mind   hind
fare   waste   bind   rind

LESSON LXXIX.

meet   duty   begun   moments
woods labor music morning

The lark is up to meet the
    sun,
The bee is on the wing;
The ant its labor has begun,
The woods with music ring.

Shall birds, and bees, and
    ants, be wise,
While I my moments waste?
Oh, let me with the morning
    rise,
And to my duty haste.

LESSON LXXX.

much
sake
your
would
able
soiled

forget   hoped   kissed
uncle   study   careful

My uncle came to see me today, and gave me this new book.

Do you see my book? I will try to study it well.

When my uncle gave it to me, he kissed me. He said

that he hoped, when he came to see me next year, he would find me able to read well.

I shall try to read well, for his sake as well as my own. I love my uncle very much.

I will try not to forget what I read in this book.

Uncle told me to be careful of my book. I shall do so, for I do not like to use books that are torn and soiled. Do you?

LESSON LXXXI.

ship   sail
mast   hail
deck   blow
wave   flow
boat   fear
float   near

cottage
chimney
window
carpet
marry
carry

LESSON LXXXII.

raker
mower
worker
working
baker
baking

sower
sowing
reaper
reaping
loading
carting

LESSON LXXXIII.

they	neck	eggs	young
these	food	swan	sticks
them	make	which	goose
large	short	hatch	months

This is a swan, which is a large bird.

It has a long neck, and short legs. It is as white as snow.

The food of the swan is the same as the food of the goose.

Swans make their nests of short sticks and grass.

Their eggs are large and white. They hatch in two months.

Did you ever see a young swan?

The young swan is not white, but it is gray.

tear	soil	found	what
hear	toil	pound	white
fear	boil	bound	while
laid	toes	would	which
paid	goes	could	where
braid	foes	should	when
whose	whole	whom	reach
	teach	peach	

LESSON LXXXIV.

ill	ate	too	has
this	pale	boy	look
been	why	cake	much

Look at this pale boy. Why is he so pale?

He has been ill. He ate too much cake.

LESSON LXXXV.

two	glad	when
felt	that	killed
days	floor	mother
ago	about	running

See this girl with her bird and cage.

She is very happy. Her kind mother gave her a new bird today.

Two days ago, the bird that she had, was running about the floor.

A cat came and killed it.

The little girl felt very sad. Now she is happy. She has another bird.

LESSON LXXXVI.

pie	nice	word	whose
stay	says	chair	fancy
dine	head	straw	master
speak	name	known	Edward

Sister Mary, come here and see Fido.

He is sitting up, and has a hat on his head.

He looks like a little boy in the chair. It is only Fido.

Shall I ask him to stay and dine with us today?

Yes, little master Fido, we are to have a very nice pig for dinner. Will you stay and take a rib with us?

If you like, you can have a bit of pie also. He says not a word.

Fido can not speak as we do, yet he has ways by which he is able to make his wants known.

Edward was the name of the boy, whose dog was Fido.

Edward was a merry, kind boy.

LESSON LXXXVII.

ones	cage	into
were	have	house
prison	other	would
birds	bush	boys
there	sorry	stolen
went	young	parents

girls   garden

One day, two boys went into a garden.

They saw a bird's nest on a rose bush.

Two little birds were in the nest.

One of the boys said,
"Let us take these birds into the house. We can put them into a cage. By and by they will sing for us."

"No," said the other boy, "birds have parents, as well as boys and girls.

"We will not take these young ones. The old birds will feel very sad.

"Our parents would be very sorry, if we were stolen and put into a prison."

LESSON LXXXVIII.

flew	knew	once
than	school	tried
been	would	table
shone	wiser	taller

I once knew a boy. He was not a big boy. If he had been a big boy, he would have been wiser. He was a little boy, not taller than the table.

One fine morning, he was sent to school. The sun shone, and the birds sang on the trees.

This little boy was not fond of studying but he was fond of playing.

This fine morning, he took a long, long time on his way to school.

He met a bee, and tried to

get it, but the bee flew away.

He met a dog too, but the dog did not stop to play with him.

When the boy got to school, it was very late.

Do you think a good boy will do as this boy did?

ECLECTIC EDUCATIONAL SERIES.

Published by W. B. Smith & Co., Cincinnati.

McGUFFEY'S ECLECTIC PRIMER,containing the Alphabet and very simple Lessons in Reading and Spelling, with numerous pictures.

McGUFFEY'S ECLECTIC SPELLING BOOK, in which is shown the exact sound of each syllable, according, to the approved principles of English Orthoepy.

McGUFFEY'S ECLECTIC FIRST READER, for the younger pupils: containing pleasing, progressive Lessons in Reading and Spelling, with numerous engravings.

McGUFFEY'S ECLECTIC SECOND READER, for young pupils containing progressive Lessons in Reading, and Spelling, with numerous engravings.

McGUFFEY'S ECLECTIC THIRD READER, for the middle classes: containing chaste and instructive Lessons in Prose and Poetry, with numerous Exercises in Defining, Enunciation, Pronunciation, &c.

McGUFFEY'S ECLECTIC FOURTH READER, for the more advanced classes: containing extracts in Prose and Poetry, from the best writers, with numerous Grammatic and other Questions, and Exercises in Enunciation, Defining, &c.

McGUFFEY'S RHETORICAL GUIDE, or FIFTH READER, a Rhetorical Reading Book for the highest classes: containing elegant extracts in Prose and Poetry, from the most classic writers, with copious Rhetorical Rules, Examples, and Notations.

THE HEMANS READER, for Female Seminaries: containing elegant extracts in Prose and Poetry, carefully selected from the writings of more than one hundred and thirty standard authors. Compiled for the Eclectic Educational Series by Dr. T. S. Pinneo.

RAY'S ARITHMETIC, PART FIRST, containing Simple Lessons for little learners, on the inductive method.

RAY'S ARITHMETIC, PART SECOND, a comprehensive and complete textbook in Mental Arithmetic.

RAY'S ARITHMETIC, PART THIRD, a simple, methodical, and complete textbook, containing copious Exercises, from the simple combination of numbers up to Geometrical Progression, Mensuration, &c. One of the most desirable Arithmetics ever published.